THE SHELTI

Dora Kennedy

Typeset and Published
by
The National Poetry Foundation
(Reg Charity No 283032)
27 Mill Road
Fareham
Hants PO16 0TH
(Tel: 0329 822218)

Printed by
Meon Valley Printers
Bishops Waltham (0489 895460)

Sponsored by Rosemary Arthur

Edited by Johnathon Clifford

Cover painting by Johnathon Clifford. *'Gatecrasher'* (4ftx3ft oils). Photographed by Ivan J Saunders L.M.P.A.

Poetry previously published in *Envoi, Wirral Journal, Lancashire Life, Poetry Nottingham, Doors, Vision On, Pause* and broadcast by BBC Radio Network Northwest.

ISBN 1 870556 92 5

CONTENTS

To my grand-daughters
Katie and Clare
for their enthusiastic support

PHOTOGRAPH
(*Grandma with bicycle*)

How this reminds me of the day
My grandma learnt to ride that bike,
It stood there gleaming on display,
Her birthday present.

Her hat was large and on the brim
A bunch of cherries bobbed about,
Her skirt was long and black and slim
Her face was grim.

We gripped the saddle tight below,
Her braided back sped down the hill,
She left the path, we let her go,
We were too slow

Or she too fast, we couldn't tell.
The holly hedge stood in her way,
We thought we heard her ring the bell
Before she fell.

She went right through, we got the blame,
Her cherry hat hung on a twig.
The bike was never quite the same.
It was a shame.

Manure heaps are soft and safe;
Discreetly screened by hedge and tree,
Sitting hidden from our sight
She was alright.

ON STRIKE

Brooding here beside the sink
it seems incredible to think
of all the meals I've served since I
was wedded and bedded.

Ham and egg and porridge oats
would reach from here to John O'Groats.
Mounds and mounds of pizza every
section   perfection.

With mugs of coffee, cups of tea,
enough to fill the Baltic Sea,
plus fish in every possible
disguise and size.

Those legs of lamb, divide by four
a flock of ninety nine or more,
that's provender to grace Belshazzar's
feast at least.

Now Christmas ninety-one has gone
with turkey number thirty-one,
Haute Cuisine for ninety-two
can stew − I'm through!

SEA SEARCH

A day to change and cloud all other days;
a boat like any other boat.
If I had known I would have called his name,
foiling the summer sea's smiling treachery.

No beach or cove they left unsearched.

Maybe the shattered hull and upturned keel deceived
and he lies snugly in some passing craft
bound for the sun.

Maybe chance blow or fever robs his mind
of sweet serenity –
to wander all unknowing and unknown –

Or lie, sea wrack, upon a distant shore.

Oh happy those who to a son's grave bring
the Christmas wreath, the flowers of early spring.

WOMEN'S CHRISTMAS LUNCH
(With apologies to Longfellow)

On the edge of lower village,
By the mighty Dee the river,
Stands the home of Eleanora
Valued member of committee;
In the house are many comforts,
Carpets spread for all to tread on
Luxury seats for all to sit in.

On the fifteenth of December
When the sun had reached its zenith,
Aided by her friend and helper
From the Hermitage beside her
She made ready for the feasting;
Soup in cauldron steaming, steaming,
Precious cut glass goblets gleaming,
Knives and forks and items sundry
For the coming of the hungry.

One by one the members gathered,
Each one bearing her own offering,
Many hours of preparation
Many thoughts and much discussion
Had been spent on these their efforts,
Trays they bore before them, laden,
Each one veiled in patterned napkin.

Came the mincepies, came the salads,
Beef and ham came, rolls and butter,
Sweets too numerous to mention,
At the last the famed Pavlova,
Quivering, quivering, as she bore it,
Dripping, dripping on her garment,
Almost lost before the feasting.

4

There they sat with well–filled glasses,
Wine from far across the water
Cheered them as they formed a circle
Clad in colours of the rainbow
Each one differing from the other.

Three times then they rose and gathered
Where the soup steamed gently, gently,
Where the food was waiting, waiting,
Where the famed Pavlova brooded,
Trifle, cheese and biscuits calling.

Red and gold, the Christmas crackers
Sparked, exploded as they pulled them,
Spilling hats and charms around them
Riddles that could not be fathomed,
And the talking and the laughter
Filled the room with warmth and gladness.

Coffee, and the feast was over;
Time to break the magic circle,
Each one took with her a portion
For the hungry waiting for them
In their houses waiting for them,
And the useful, mighty Hoover
With a noise, a sound like thunder
Cleared the crumbs from off the carpet,
Carpet spread for all to walk on.

CARVED HORSE

This figure was the last she carved,
her gelding Tawny-mane.
Choosing the pine – form, colour –
all must be true; such beauty in a beast
called for the best. See how the grain
pursues a line from neck to nostril,
how wind lifts the mane.
For her alone he lowered his head 'just so'
in welcome; eager for her voice, her touch.
She said, "Achilles' steeds were not so fine
before the walls of Troy and they, god-given."

We could not know that as they mourned
their charioteer, so he would mourn for her.

FLYING OUT OF VANCOUVER

I hate this moment when the plane
is making up its mind to fly,
disasters flash before my eyes
I know the thing will never rise –
at last we're up and flying out to sea.
To sea? Now that seems wrong to me;
I thought Europe was over there
behind the Rockies; I wonder if
the pilot knows we're heading for Japan.
The steward says we're gaining height
and everything will be alright;
I'm sure my wing has fallen off, it's missing.

In one great arc we soar around
(my stomach feels it's outward bound)
ice caps loom before us, near, too near!
We climb and climb and climb again –
whatever made me join this tour
we're going to hit that peak for sure?
The man beside me points below
"A plane once crashed right here, you know
too high to take the bodies down –"
The Clown!
I cry "Help! Help! Oh stop the plane
I'll never never fly again, I want to *get off*."

"Get off?" he says, "Now that's absurd,
take my advice; order a double whisky – twice –
before the breakfast trays come round."

YEW TREES AT SPEKE HALL

They dominate the courtyard
these great yews, Adam and Eve,
survivors of a thousand years;
seeded when wooded land and
settlement still lay in Saxon hands;
four centuries before these walls
were built.

Half–timbered, moulded and carved,
beloved, neglected, torn by civil
war and now restored, the essence
of this house lives on.
No stately edifice – a home set
in smooth lawns, scented by roses
and small enough to love.

"The story goes," its guardian said
(indulgent to our ignorance) "he
gambled it away, that profligate
descendant of Nell Gwynne – and she
his wife, last of that long line
and loving it so well declared,
'I'll never leave this place.'

From some such height as this
she let the baby fall and followed
it herself.
Through this small window in the
panelling the priest hole can be
seen, concealed beside the chimney
breast . . ."

Above the yews planes fly low
taking passengers to Speke airport.

IF ONLY

Two paths to school,
Taking the road way
Between hazel hedges
Over the common,
Geese lay in ambush.

Taking the field way
Past the old walnut
Red and white heifers
Lurked in the hollow.

Whichever was chosen then
Seemed the wrong way,
Setting a pattern
Ever repeated.

The spade was made of wood
the pail a gift
from Cow and Gate;
the train puffed on.
I cried, "The sea! The sea!"
and gave the pail a whack,
passengers drew back – fled.
"I'm not surprised, " she said;
"Look, we're almost there –"

The train screeched!
Ducks and drakes flew like mad,
"Those ducks are gulls," she said,
(her feet had knobs on every toe)
"You've soaked my skirt," she said,
"Sit down, the sandwiches
are full of sand."
"Build me a castle ten feet high,"
"It's time to go," she said.

TELL ME

Oh streaking
smoke–grey   stranger,
skimpy tail outstretched .
flying along fences
appearing, disappearing –
Bird–table bandit
robber of robins
saboteur of saplings
tell me,
what envious elfin ploy
has stolen away my brown
bushy–tailed   beauty
and left a changeling
in its place?

CHERRY TREE

Some vandal in our road
chopped down his cherry tree;
seal–brown bark butchered,
buds (pregnant with promise)
crushed
by careless feet.

He sunbathes now
where delicate clusters hung.

Under his feet
the dark life force,
robbed of branches,
vitalises roots,
seethes into suckers,
lifts paths and flagstones
in revenge.

CRETAN VASE
(*The Bull Leaper*)

This youth who stands,
Immortalised by a potter's art
Beside the double-headed axe;
Was he one of that tribute paid
When Theseus braved King Minos' wrath
And slew the dreaded Minotaur?

Was it he, when sailing home
Triumphant with Prince Theseus,
Who left the sable sail unchanged,
Bringing King Aegeus to his grave
And leaving this, his image, for posterity?

SPRING TIDE IN THE DEE ESTUARY

This is an occasion; today
the tide is due at Parkgate.
Once an every day affair
with ships sailing to Dublin,
now a phenomenon, conjured up
by strong winds and a spring tide.
We say, "All on one side like Parkgate"
and so it is; massed dwellings,
its famous school on this side,
on the other wild marshes stretch
towards the slopes of Wales.

Spectators line what used to be the quay,
(inclement weather, records say,
prevented Handel from embarking here
with his Messiah). Pools form
and a skim of water covers grass and sedge.
Over the sea—wall children, armed
with sticks, attempt to rescue mice
marooned on flotsam.
Catcall after a solitary rat, slinking
half—immersed in scum.
Pose for photographs —
with sandbanks submerged birds
stream in to the sanctuary.

Water deepens but the influx is brief;
unobtrusively the tide recedes,
visitors resume their promenade,
old cottages laze in the sun.
Among the cobbles *Nelson* is spelt out
in black round stones.
Is it a tribute to the great man,
dallying maybe with his Emma,
the blacksmith's daughter from Ness
just up the road?
A local lad enlightens us –
a child, a boy, lost like Kingsley's
Mary, who went to call the cattle home
across these hidden sands.

As tides go it is a poor show
but we are satisfied,
today we saw the tide in at Parkgate.

DILEMMA

Oh who would marry a long-boat man,
Bold eyes (a Mediterranean tan)
Laughing, teasing, spoiling to fight
Lads of the town on Saturday night.
Peddling goods (Hong Kong, Japan)
Oh who would marry a long-boat man?

Oh who would be a long-boat wife,
Baskets and pegs (Lord, what a life!)
Coals and timber, country store,
Carried and carted from door to door.
Bundles and babies, women and strife,
Oh who would be a long-boat wife?

It was Spring, young leaves and evening mist.
Clover, deep, where we met and kissed;
Oh I would give the world away
To marry the long-boat man today.

PIT STOP
(Appeal to a car addict)

Don't be an impatient patient,
Don't grudge your visitors a grape,
I see they've got you fast, immobile; will it last?
They've labelled you with little bits of tape.

Don't shoot the pianist when he's playing
Even if he cracks a rib or two,
He really does his best and if you'll only *rest*
He'll have you on your feet as good as new.

Don't try slipstreaming in the wheelchair
And don't take the ambulance apart:
Remember if you please, we've all worn out our knees
Praying while that lot decoked your heart.

SPIRIT OF LIVERPOOL
(Aerial sculpture in the Cathedral Church of Christ)

Above the city, from St. James's Mount,
this latest Cathedral looks down upon an idle river,
silent docks and cranes static against a clear sky;
the largest in Britain and fifth in all the world.

Enriched by Autumn–gilded leaves, red sandstone walls
soar into arch and tower – a hymn of praise –
dreamed and created by an architect of twenty two.

Today in the western transept,
against a sapphire backdrop of stained glass,
players rehearse their parts. Tudor dignitaries
pose and gesture, declaim their accusations;
Sir Thomas More, with passion, reiterates allegiance
to an older faith and is condemned.

The Mariner's bell chimes! Above the clock,
delicate sculptured sails change from white to peach,
through pale yellow to green – and revert.
Here, time has put the old constraints to rest;
Catholic and Anglican Cathedrals share this street
called Hope, in perfect amity.

CAT AND DOG LIFE

The armistice is frail and often broken;
encroachment on each other's dish
enough to start a war and banishment
for both! Weapons are crude, reduced
to a minimum; hustle and noise on his side,
spitting and sheathed claws on hers.
To him the stairs are out of bounds,
half way she lies idly tantalizing
through bannisters; his chance comes
with the cat–flap, that moment when
her back is turned –
She spends her time roaming the fields,
he is confined; his habit of leaping
five barred gate and fence deplored.

Formidable when united they defend each
inch of ground – venerate the same gods.

AFTER SNOW

After the snow had gone
I walked timidly
like a stranger;
cautiously testing
for ice traps
among debris –
empty bottles
take–away cartons,
now unmercifully
revealed.

When suddenly
I heard you say
"Steady, girl, steady,"
and felt
(for one short second)
your hand in mine
just long enough
to send me
stumbling home.

PLAYTIME

When they dug up bones
looking for drains
everything in the playground
stopped.

Fearsome they looked
all laid out;
the foreman bawled
"Clear off you kids"
and Miss rang for class
five minutes early.

Evans twins went home,
queasy, they said,
we knew different!
With plums ripe
and Ben Bowcott at market
they'd have jam made by tea.

An old graveyard,
Vicar said, and
to leave them in peace.
Seventeenth century they were;
I put my bit back,
too old for our Lassie.

RAIN DRAIN

It seems a shame to sit in that old school
when ditch is overflowing and the pool
is full of fishes waiting for a bite –
it don't seem right.

There's thirty of us in our class, I guess
no–one will notice if there's just one less;
I've borrowed sandwiches and Gran's fruit scone,
these wellies I've got on

have waited all the summer to be wet
right to the top. Why do we only get
floods when a fellow's fast on the rein
swotting?

My mum says, "If you're tempted to be bad
sit down and listen to your conscience, lad;"
I've sat 'till bottom's numb beneath this tree.
It said – "O.K. Be back for tea."

CHILD'S EYE VIEW

At Eastertide my father died –

Lilies marching round his bed,
Two brief candles at his head,
Hooded windows peering, mourners,
Relatives in drifts, in corners,
Whispering, whispering, "Up at dawn
On Saturday he mowed the lawn."

Two farm horses; teasing flies;
Black alpaca scratching thighs,
Wagon wheels picked out in red,
Solemn Requiem for the dead.
He lies where yew tree shadows fall
And does not hear me when I call.

THE STREAM

It was never more than ankle-deep
Just there —
Pebbly,
Quicksilvered with minnows,
Water-meadows, scarred by rushes,
Stretched on either side.

To us he was the quiet one,
Inventor of games,
A peacemaker;
We missed him when they moved away,
Quarrels seemed deeper
More lasting.

They said he did well there
In the city.
Why then, so long after, did he come back
For that?

It was never more than ankle-deep
Just there —
Who would have thought it deep enough
To drown?

RACISM

Earthbound,
Flight feathers trailing,
The magpie in the garden
Drags a glossy broken wing;
A morning–coated reveller
Reduced to penury.
Cannibal!
I detest this brassy breed
And yet, in pity,
Can neither see it starve
Nor commit the fatal deed.

Starlings in the roof,
Whose hobnailed forays
Start at earliest light,
Are not so tolerant;
They mob it on sight.

STRAY LAYER

"Keep an eye on the Black Leghorn," they say
commanding the impossible.

Delicately side–stepping
she deliberates over nesting boxes,
scorns the lure of china eggs,
protests querulously
as she sets off for the field.
I follow her scarlet beret through the grass.

We have played this game before;
she is striking a blow for freedom,
tired of family planning.

She will never sit on eggs
she's the wrong shape.
They will choose Sussex
or Wyandottes with their wide expanse
of feather bloomers.

She makes for the great ditch,
ankle deep in mud and primroses,
its pits (unmarked) dumps for kitchen rubbish –
I hesitate; she vanishes.

From crannies further on, she cackles
triumphantly announcing a safe delivery.
Last spring she brought home nine chicks,
beady-eyed trouble-makers like herself;
I shake a fist in her direction.

"I hope they're all addled," I shout.
"I hope the fox gets you."

CHARTED BY EELS

With no sea for miles
it became our playground,
heavenly cool to sun–scorched limbs
bitten by harvesters.

It had its own set of rules
keeping short stretches shallow,
polishing pebbles,
manoeuvreing minnows,
safe for siblings.

Round bends it played tricks
with whirlpools.

After heavy rain it cheated;
undermined trees,
scoured out banks,
set new traps
charted by eels.

In winter it flooded,
inundating fields
damming narrows with dead sheep –
or worse.

Each spring it laid carpets,
starred with blossom,
on dangerous deeps.

It never pretended it could be trusted.

KILLING TIME

Each October brought a new one,
delicately pink, solidly plump,
tittuping on small trotters,
tail a perpetual question mark.

"Cleaner than a dog around the place,"
the woman said,
"given a chance."

"Old Joey's gone to a Better Home,"
the children chanted,
thrusting New Joey into battered pram,
cramming baby bonnet over flinching ears.

We pictured him
lording it over a proper sty,
scavenging under opulent tables,
blessing other kitchens
with satisfied grunts.

We barely noticed
the smoking of hams,
hooks laden with flitches.

Only in dreams did the screams intrude.

BEFORE MYXOMATOSIS

There were so many,
Honeycombing bare hillsides,
White scuts skittering,
Gipsy fare; but relished.

Unmoved we saw them brought in,
Hind legs strung together,
Nostrils dripping blood;
Survival to the fleetest.

We never grudged them
Their forays
Into the cornfield,
Until the harvest –

All day the combine
Cutting, binding, ejecting;
All day the timid retreating
Before the blades.

It was that last small square
Broke the heart;
Overflowing, rippling with life,
Nowhere to go
Except out towards the waiting circle –
Men. Guns. Dogs.

BINGO BRIDES

Eager as brides they gather at bus stops,
(Fine feathers – hairdos straight from *The Street*)
Waiting for the two fifteen, ready to do battle
At Eyes Down, Three P.M. Mon. Wed. and Sat.

They chat up every driver on the route.
"Get a move on, Lad," they say scoring first point.
"Is no-one paying?" He demands as
Passes flash before his eyes.

Attached five-year-old photos show
Small resemblance to present bearers;
Shades of hair, startling discrepancies.
"A right Rogues Gallery," he announces.

"You can laugh! Six hundred of your lot
Fell off their perches last year and
What became of their passes? Tell me that!
Twenty pounds a-piece in Liverpool pubs."

They scream a protest as he revs up –
Pretends to pass their regular stop;
Strident as starlings they muster for flight,
Swoop through illuminated doors to heaven.

THE TIGER

In Liverpool, in Water Street,
Where East and Western cultures meet,
There stands a Bank and on the door
With curving tongue, with yawning jaw,
No neck, no leg, no tail, no paw,
A tiger's head with one bright fang
Looks down towards the sea.

Here gentlemen from Mandalay,
Pakistan, or far Cathay
(China as we say today)
Come searching, searching up the street
And at the massive door they pause
And each with slender olive hand
Touches the shining tooth.

Now it is said that fortune fair
Favours those who linger there,
That nostrils wide and slitted eyes
Are benefactors in disguise
To those who touch that tiger's fang,
But I have tried for all to see
And nothing came to me.

THE OTHER SIDE

As children do
we knew the common well,
had plaited its rushes
transported its frogs
raced snails on sour patches
fled in mock-terror from
the strong-winged gander
and his flock.

That bitter winter morning,
the Lugg overflowing
and ditches frost-locked,
it stretched like a sheet of silver
scarred by the tips of rushes
and a narrowing gap
where the tramp's cap
floated . . .

THE OWL

They have felled the tree where the great owl sat
by the Norman tower
and who will watch over the old graveyard
at the witching hour?
The blade in the bough bit deep and hard
with a whining power
two hundred years of growth and more
cut like a flower.

And who will watch the moon rise high
where the willows weep
or wake small furry things that lie
deep in sleep?
Who will keep guard in the lonely night
on the blesséd dead
for the tree has been felled where the great owl called
and the wise one fled?

MY BROTHER

His hair was thick and red;
swirling round and round
in the whirlpool's grip,
it looked like grazing trout
dipping and surfacing;
we watched from where we stood
in sun-warmed shallows.

My father, towel in hand,
was dressed and waiting.
He ran and dived
where the water crawled
green-deep in scoured bed.
"He'll catch it when
my mother comes, " I said.

Smiling she came down the field,
at the river's brink she screamed
and flung up basket, cake
and lemonade.
"Dear Lord," she said
but didn't bow her head.

Father seized the mat of hair
and dragged him to the bank;
my brother lay face down –
He threw up muddy water,
water-weed and groaned.
"If he dies," I thought,
"his new bat will be mine."

He rode home pick-a-back
across the meadow,
I said, "I'm glad you didn't
die," and gave him my
three-bladed knife.
I cared nothing for his stupid bat,
a brother lasts for life.

CHILD'S PLAY
(Only pretending Gran)

Today the children came
and life became alive!
Hot scones and sausages
and "Leave the dishes Gran
the hairdresser is here."
I'm washed and trimmed,
pinned up, dried, combed
and drenched in Chanel No. 5
(a treasured birthday treat).

Like magic I become
Miss Mott, teacher of gym;
we march, skip, hop,
knees bend each time
the whistle blows – "No dear
I cannot touch my toes.
Home now children, don't be late
Mother's waiting at the gate."

Shortage of cast compels
and in another room
I am the mother,
welcoming them home
with orange juice
and jaffa cakes –
but time is running on.

I am a casualty
like Granny White
who crossed on the red light;
I am tucked up, admonished,
fed with milky tea,
dosed well with smarties
I miraculously revive
in time to wave goodbye.

Today the children came
filling all my stage,
and those regrets that time
and sorrow bring retreated,
defeated, into the wings.

TRIAL BY PEERS

Quiet, he said, be quiet,
Let a fellow speak;
Let him get it off his chest
Or we'll be here half the week.

He threw her in the river
We're all agreed on that;
He must have had good reason
Or was it tit for tat?

If Joe here hadn't seen her
She'd be in the past tense,
But as she's here and fighting fit,
There doesn't seem much sense

In prisoning up a fellow,
It's just the truth we seek,
Did it happen absent minded like?
Let the fellow speak.

Quiet, she said, be quiet,
Hear what I have to say,
Though he was a trifle hasty
He's apologised today,

I've been courting him a long time
And at last he's had to speak,
He don't want to go to prison
So he's wedding me next week.

BARE HOLLOWS

Easier now to plough
this hedge–stripped field,
no hawthorn bough sweeps low
to slow the blade;
no bustling thrush,
no brood in the thorn,
only bare hollows
where rude hands have torn
this living chart,
custodian of long years,
apart.

No more a brief retreat
for foundering feet –
Where will the blackbird nest,
the vagrant rest?

THE CONWAY BELL

Do you remember the Conway
How sweetly she rose to the swell
And the Conway Boys like clockwork toys
And the sound of the Conway bell?

To and fro on the ferry,
Caught in a magic spell
Of mast and spar and rigging we sailed
To the urgent calling bell.

The never ending pacing
To the engine's rhythmic pound,
Would pause as we passed the Conway
And wait to catch the sound.

They towed her away from the Mersey,
They took her out of our care;
How could we bear to cross to school
And our own ship not there?

Beyond the Lightship Bar she sailed,
Beyond the Rip Rap buoy,
In Menai Strait to an alien shore
They moored our pride and joy.

She never returned to the river,
They let her drift away,
She broke her back, we broke our hearts
And there she lies today.

Oh I remember the Conway,
Remember the tears that fell,
For part of childhood's magic fled
With the Conway bell.

PROWLER

Scent his betrayer,
at one with the night,
he is here.

Old dog grumbles
pointing   windward.

Behind stable doors
iron—shod hooves strike,
igniting jittery hens
to panic –
clucking,   cackling,
a windrushing of feathers.

Stealthily
he probes mesh and bolt;
foiled, he glides,
shadow into shadow,
trailing behind him
the sly rank smell . . .

PAPER BOATS

How can I tell you when I miss him most?
Perhaps when cars speed homeward from the shore
And small boats run towards the sheltering coast,
I wait and know that he will come no more.

Or when in early dawn bemused by sleep,
Whose gentle fingers from my mind erase
For one short moment memory of my grief;
I hold out hands, in love, to touch his face.

In crowded rooms a turn of head; a trace
Of April sunlight where the birches stand,
Shop windows, wedding rings and bridal lace –
Paper boats and castles made of sand;

For each and all of these the tears will start,
Foolish betrayers of a foolish heart.